# DODD, MEAD WONDERS BOOKS

WONDERS OF ALLIGATORS AND CROCODILES by Wyatt Blassingame
WONDERS OF ANIMAL ARCHITECTURE by Sigmund A. Lavine
WONDERS OF ANIMAL NURSERIES by Jacquelyn Berrill
WONDERS OF BARNACLES by Arnold Ross and William K. Emerson
WONDERS OF THE BAT WORLD by Sigmund A. Lavine
WONDERS BEYOND THE SOLAR SYSTEM by Rocco Feravolo
WONDERS OF THE BISON WORLD by Sigmund A. Lavine and Vincent Scuro
WONDERS OF THE CACTUS WORLD by Sigmund A. Lavine
WONDERS OF CARIBOU by Jim Rearden
WONDERS OF THE DINOSAUR WORLD by William H. Matthews III
WONDERS OF THE EAGLE WORLD by Sigmund A. Lavine
WONDERS OF THE FLY WORLD by Sigmund A. Lavine
WONDERS OF FROGS AND TOADS by Wyatt Blassingame
WONDERS OF GEESE AND SWANS by Thomas D. Fegely
WONDERS OF GEMS by Richard M. Pearl
WONDERS OF GRAVITY by Rocco Feravolo
WONDERS OF THE HAWK WORLD by Sigmund A. Lavine
WONDERS OF HERBS by Sigmund A. Lavine
WONDERS OF HUMMINGBIRDS by Hilda Simon
WONDERS OF THE KELP FOREST by Joseph E. Brown
WONDERS OF LLAMAS by Roger Perry
WONDERS OF LIONS by George and Kay Schaller
WONDERS OF MATHEMATICS by Rocco Feravolo
WONDERS OF MEASUREMENT by Owen S. Lieberg
WONDERS OF THE MONKEY WORLD by Jacquelyn Berrill
WONDERS OF THE MOSQUITO WORLD by Phil Ault
WONDERS OF THE OWL WORLD by Sigmund A. Lavine
WONDERS OF THE PELICAN WORLD by Joseph J. Cook and Ralph W. Schreiber
WONDERS OF PRAIRIE DOGS by G. Earl Chace
WONDERS OF THE PRONGHORN by G. Earl Chace
WONDERS OF RACCOONS by Wyatt Blassingame
WONDERS OF ROCKS AND MINERALS by Richard M. Pearl
WONDERS OF SAND by Christie McFall
WONDERS OF SEA GULLS by Elizabeth Anne and Ralph W. Schreiber
WONDERS OF SEALS AND SEA LIONS by Joseph E. Brown
WONDERS OF SOUND by Rocco Feravolo
WONDERS OF THE SPIDER WORLD by Sigmund A. Lavine
WONDERS OF SPONGES by Morris K. Jacobson and Rosemary K. Pang
WONDERS OF STARFISH by Morris K. Jacobson and William K. Emerson
WONDERS OF STONES by Christie McFall
WONDERS OF TERRARIUMS by Sigmund A. Lavine
WONDERS OF THE TREE WORLD by Margaret Cosgrove
WONDERS OF THE TURTLE WORLD by Wyatt Blassingame
WONDERS OF WILD DUCKS by Thomas D. Fegely
WONDERS OF THE WOODS AND DESERT AT NIGHT by Jacquelyn Berrill
WONDERS OF THE WORLD OF THE ALBATROSS by Harvey and Mildred Fisher
WONDERS OF THE WORLD OF BEARS by Bernadine Bailey
WONDERS OF THE WORLD OF HORSES by Sigmund A. Lavine and Brigid Casey
WONDERS OF THE WORLD OF SHELLS by Morris K. Jacobson and
    William K. Emerson
WONDERS OF THE WORLD OF WOLVES by Jacquelyn Berrill
WONDERS OF YOUR SENSES by Margaret Cosgrove

# WONDERS OF RACCOONS

## Wyatt Blassingame

Illustrated with photographs

DODD, MEAD & COMPANY,  NEW YORK

PICTURE CREDITS

"Snooks" Adams, 57; Wyatt Blassingame, 11, 26, 31 (bottom), 35, 78; Florida Audubon Society, 15; Florida Game & Fresh Water Fish Commission, 2 (by Bob Brantly), 16 (top), 16 (bottom left) (by Steve Theg), 23 (by Wallace Hughes), 24 (by Jim Floyd), 33 (by Wallace Hughes), 48 (by Lovett Williams), 63 (by Gene Smith), 64 (by Jim Floyd); Florida News Bureau, 16 (bottom right); New Jersey Division of Fish & Game, 40, 67; New York State Department of Environmental Conservation, 46, 76, 77 (left); New York Zoological Society Photo, 69; Dave Norris, 8, 17, 20, 55; Gene Page, Photographic Infinity, Inc., 21, 29, 51, 53, 58, 61, 75, 77 (right); Leonard Lee Rue III, 31 (top), 37, 39, 44, 72; and Texas Parks & Wildlife Department, 71.

Library of Congress Cataloging in Publication Data

Blassingame, Wyatt.
    Wonders of raccoons.

    Includes index.
    SUMMARY: Discusses the characteristics, habits, and
behavior of the raccoon, a very adaptable animal native
to North America.
    1. Raccoons—Juvenile literature.   [1. Raccoons]
I. Title.
QL737.C26B58        599'.74443        77–6491
ISBN 0–396–07485–5

FOR TED JACKSON
who may have a pet raccoon of his own, one of these days

# Contents

*A full-grown raccoon*

# 1. A National Animal

If the United States should ever choose a national mammal, it ought to be the raccoon.

Raccoons were here long before the first white man. They are native to all the mainland forty-eight states, to the countries closely bordering them, and to nowhere else. And from the very first of our recorded history, they have played a large role in that history.

In 1608, when Captain John Smith visited the Indian Chief Powhatan, he found the chief sitting "before a fire upon a seat like a bedstead . . . with a great robe made of raccoon skins, and all the tails hanging by." In fact it was Captain John Smith who wrote the first English description of the raccoon. The Indians, he said, had "a beast . . . much like a badger, but useth to live on trees as squirrels do."

The Indians called this animal, Smith said, *aroughcum*, a word meaning that it felt or scratched with its hands. It was an excellent name with an accurate meaning, as we will see. But Captain Smith and his fellow Englishmen soon shortened the word to raccoon, or just coon. Scientists now call it *Procyon lotor*, which is not nearly as fitting a name as the Indian one. But more about that later.

In 1743 a man named John Brickell wrote what he thought to be the first detailed description of the animal.

9

The *Raccoon* (which I take to be a species of the *Monkey*) is of a dark gray colour, and shape and bigness partly resembles a *Fox*, but has large black Eyes with Whiskers like a Cat, the Nose like a *Pig*, and the Feet are form'd like a Hand or those of a *Monkey*.

Up to this point Brickell's description was rather accurate. But then he went on to describe what he believed to be its way of feeding.

This Animal is very fond of *Crabs*, which are plenty in this Province, and the way they take them is remarkable and diverting, for when it intends to make a prey of this Fish, he goes to the Marshes on the Water side, and standing on the Land he lets his tail hang down in the water, which the *Crab* takes for a bait, and fastens his claws therein; as soon as the *Raccoon* perceives it, he of a sudden springs forward a considerable way on the Land, and brings the *Crab* with him; as soon as the *Crab* finds himself out of his Element, he immediately lets go of his hold, and then the *Raccoon* encounters him by getting him cross-ways in his mouth, and so devours him.

No one since Brickell's time has ever reported seeing a raccoon catch crabs in this way. But quite possibly it could have happened. Coons certainly hunt for crabs and small fish along the edges of lakes, rivers, and even the seashore, dragging their tails in the water behind them. And maybe a crab has grabbed one. If it did, quite certainly the raccoon would jump, dragging the crab with it.

But even if no one ever saw a raccoon use its tail for crab bait, the early settlers, like the Indians before them, knew the animal well. They ate its flesh when hungry and made robes, coats, and hats from its skin. Long before Davy Crockett or Daniel Boone,

10

*The Davy Crockett raccoon skin cap is very popular with young hunters.*

the coonskin cap was a badge of the wilderness hunter. As settlers moved westward, creating new frontiers, they used the fat of raccoons to grease their boots and wagon wheels. They boiled it to make lard for their lamps. They used the skins in place of money. Along the frontier where actual money was scarce, a man might be, and often was, paid in raccoon skins. In what is now eastern Tennessee the official salary of members of the state assembly was three raccoon skins a day while in session.

### RACCOON FOLK TALES

Both the Indians and the frontiersmen had their raccoon legends. Most of them dealt with tricks of one kind or another, because raccoons themselves just seem to be natural tricksters, born comedians.

One of the Indian stories is about a raccoon hunting for crayfish along the edge of a lake. It came upon a rope, one end of which was tied to a rock in the water. The other end of the rope

11

led to a tepee in which two blind Indians lived. While the raccoon watched, one of the Indians took a bucket and started following the rope, planning to get water from the lake.

The raccoon quickly untied the rope from the rock in the water and tied it to another on dry land. The blind man came to the end of the rope, felt around, and found no water. He went back to the tepee. "The lake has dried up," he said.

"You're crazy," the other Indian said. He took the bucket and followed the rope. Again the raccoon untied the end and retied it to the rock in the lake. The blind Indian came to the water, filled his bucket, and went back to the tepee. "I told you that you were crazy," he said.

"There must have been a heavy rain," the first Indian said.

This story goes on with the raccoon playing one trick after another on the two Indians. Finally they began to fight. But when they heard the coon laughing—and coons can come very close to laughing, just as they can untie ropes—the Indians knew they had been tricked.

In some stories the raccoon is used by human tricksters. The great author Mark Twain told such a story about his own boyhood. He and another boy needed money, Twain said, but their only possession was an old, moth-eaten raccoon skin. They took it to a country store and the owner, feeling sorry for them, gave them a dime. Then he threw the skin into a back room near a rear window. While one boy stood lookout, the other reached in and got the skin. They took it back in the store, and sold it again. The trick worked so well they played it again. And again. Until finally the store owner looked in the back room where he had been throwing coonskins all afternoon—and all he saw was one skin and a twelve-year-old boy reaching for it.

Actually this story had been told a thousand times or more before Mark Twain told it. It was an old joke along the frontier. Davy Crockett had told one version of it about himself. When frontiersmen wanted to make jokes, they often used the raccoon as part of the story.

When the American frontier disappeared, many animals disappeared with it. But not the raccoon. There are probably as many raccoons in the country today as when Davy Crockett used their skins for caps. Among the smartest, most attractive, and most common of all wild American animals, raccoons are well worth knowing about.

# 2. The Adaptable Raccoon

Many species of animals need a highly specialized environment in which to survive. If man or nature alters this environment, the animal is endangered, perhaps wiped out. The Everglades kite, for instance, feeds only on a certain species of large, freshwater snail that lives in semitropical climates. But pollution and the draining of freshwater marshes have limited the areas in which these snails survive. The Everglades kite has been unable to change its eating habits. Today it is almost extinct.

Whooping cranes will nest only in a wilderness of shallow ponds and thick brush. When civilization turned many of these areas into farms and towns, the whooping cranes could not adapt themselves to new nesting grounds. Today there are less than one hundred whooping cranes alive, all nesting in one area of northwestern Canada.

But the raccoon is adaptable. As the American environment has changed, the raccoon has changed with it. At one time chestnut trees grew thickly over much of the eastern United States. And chestnuts then made up a good part of the raccoon's autumn diet. But when disease killed off most of the chestnut trees, it did not kill off the coons. They turned to eating acorns, the fruit of the huckleberry, wild plums, whatever was available. Nor do raccoons limit themselves to vegetable matter. They feed on fish, frogs, insects, baby birds, eggs. The list is

*Frogs make up a good part of the raccoon's diet, particularly in spring and summer.*

endless, depending largely on what the raccoon can find.

The raccoon can adjust his living habits as well as his eating habits. If farmers or real estate developers cut down the hollow tree in which he normally lives, he finds another home. It may be under a rock fence, the underground burrow of another animal, somebody's attic, or whatever tree—hollow or not—has been left standing.

I live on an island off the Gulf Coast of Florida. Years ago when I first came here there were very few people, but very many coons. They nested chiefly in the tops of cabbage palms. They ate the berries of the palms and hunted for fish and crabs along the marshy bayous. Then came a real estate boom. Many of the palms were cut down. The marshes were drained and filled. Houses went up everywhere. Now we have many people —and many raccoons. The coons still nest in the tops of the palms, even if the palm is in somebody's front yard. If a home-owner leaves the island to go north for a summer, he is quite likely, on returning, to find a family of coons in his attic. With the marshes gone, the raccoons hunt along the edges of man-made canals. If the canals are seawalled, making it impossible for the coons to wade in shallow water, they simply turn to nearby garbage cans.

Bobcats will kill and eat young raccoons. But once the raccoon is mature, not even a bobcat wants to give battle.

The great horned owl (left) can catch and kill baby raccoons. The alligator (below) is one of the few animals that can catch and eat a fully grown raccoon.

The raccoon is so adaptable there is no wonder it has managed to survive in a changing environment. The wonder is that the whole country isn't waist deep in coons. They have few natural enemies. Bobcats and owls will eat the baby raccoons, but neither bobcat nor owl is anxious to attack a fully grown, sharp-toothed, long-clawed raccoon. Alligators will eat them, given a chance. But alligators get few chances, even in the limited territory shared by both animals.

Healthy raccoons have an average life span of ten to twelve years. This is often shortened by disease, a shortage of food, or both. In its natural wild state the raccoon population will sometimes become too great for the food supply. A long drought will

*Raccoons, like dogs and cats, get fleas, ticks, and other parasites.*

dry up the marshes where it hunts for frogs and fish. An unusually cold winter, or heavy snow, may make finding food impossible. Under these conditions many raccoons will starve. Or, weakened by hunger, they may die of disease. Coons suffer from both dog and cat distemper. Many parasites, both internal and external, feed on them, because coons, despite their habit of playing in the water, are not clean animals. Coons may have pneumonia, tetanus, and other diseases. Sometimes an epidemic of rabies will almost wipe out an entire raccoon population.

Even so, in many places it is man and the man-made automobile that are the raccoon's worst enemies. Where raccoons have moved into suburban areas it is probable that more are killed by automobiles than by hunger, disease, and old age put together.

# 3. Long-tailed Bear into Washing Star

It was the great Swedish scientist Carl Linnaeus who first devised a system of giving exact, scientific names to plants and animals. This was necessary because the same plant or animal might have a dozen different common names in different parts of the world. Under Linnaeus' system each thing would have a first name that would tell what genus of plants or animals it belonged to. There would be a second, or even a third or fourth, name to describe the exact species.

In 1747, Linnaeus gave the raccoon its first scientific name: *Ursus cauda elongata*, meaning "long-tailed bear."

At this time it is doubtful that Linnaeus had ever actually seen a raccoon. Perhaps he never did. (Remember, they are native to America and nowhere else.) But Linnaeus had heard about them. He had been told they looked like small bears with long tails. They climbed trees as bears did. In cold climates they slept for long periods during the winter, and bears did also. The raccoon had plantigrade feet; that is, the coon walked on the whole sole of its foot just as men, and bears, do. Also, its hind legs were longer than its front legs, so that it walked with an odd, bearlike shuffle.

Linnaeus quite naturally decided that the raccoon belonged to the bear family. His scientific name for the bear was *Ursus*

*People once believed that the raccoon belonged to the bear family.*

*cauda abrupta,* "short-tailed bear." And so the raccoon became *Ursus cauda elongata.*

A few years later Linnaeus either saw or was told more about raccoons. They had a curious habit of washing all their food before eating. (Actually the raccoon does not wash all its food, but we'll get to that in more detail later.) So in the 1758 edition of *Systema Naturae,* his book about the scientific naming of plants and animals, Linnaeus called the raccoon *Ursus lotor,* meaning "washing bear."

By this time more and more raccoons were being sent to European zoos. People stared at them, fascinated. They watched them dip food in water and rub it between their fingers before eating. Soon the common German name for the raccoon became *waschbar*, washing bear. In Sweden, the common name was *tvättbjorn*, *tvätt* for washing, *bjorn* for bear.

But as more animals were brought to Europe and European scientists made more detailed anatomical studies, they decided the creature, by whatever common name it was called, did not really belong to the bear family. Gottlieb Storr, a German scientist, gave it a new scientific name. He called it *Procyon lotor*.

The *lotor* still meant "washing," but just why Storr chose the name *Procyon* is a mystery. *Procyon* is the Greek name for a double star that rises just before Sirius, the Dog Star. Maybe Storr was thinking of the raccoon as the forefather of the dog. Today scientists do not connect the raccoon with the dog or with any other animal very closely. It is a family of its own. But Gottlieb Storr's name has stuck, and the raccoon is still *Procyon lotor*.

*Raccoons sometimes wash their food before eating. This one loves to play in the water.*

# 4. The Masked Bandit

When you look at a raccoon, or even a picture of a raccoon, probably the first thing you notice is that it's wearing a black mask like that of a bandit. But even with its mask, the raccoon doesn't look very threatening. Instead, it looks cute. There's no other word for it. Its face is long, slightly fox-shaped. Its ears stand straight up. Its round, black nose looks as if it were made of putty, like that of a circus clown. Long whiskers stand out on each side of its nose. Behind the mask its eyes are round, pitch black, and stare at you without blinking. The whole face looks like that of a very small child dressed to go trick or treating on Halloween.

The size of a fully grown raccoon will vary not only from one animal to another, but also in different parts of the country. On the whole, northern raccoons are slightly larger than southern raccoons. On an average they will stand about nine to twelve inches high at the shoulder. (Since the back legs are slightly longer than the front legs, the coon's hips are higher than its shoulders.) The average weight is about twelve to sixteen pounds. Raccoons have been reported to weigh fifty pounds and even more, but this would be a most unusual animal. Also, it would be in the autumn when they become very fat.

Whatever its weight, the raccoon is amazingly strong for its

*Raccoons have black masks, which make them look like bandits.*

*Raccoons can climb trees very easily.*

size. Dr. Leon Whitney, a scientist who studied raccoons for many years, once tried to pull one out of a hollow tree. The coon was clutching the tree with all four legs. Dr. Whitney pulled on its tail. He pulled so hard he lifted himself clear off the ground without budging the coon. And Dr. Whitney weighed two hundred pounds!

Raccoons are not only strong, they are agile. They can run up and down trees, or along small tree limbs like squirrels. Usually a coon goes up a tree headfirst and comes down tailfirst, but not always. If for some reason a mother coon decides to move her babies from one hollow tree to another, she usually comes down the tree headfirst carrying a baby with the scruff of its neck clutched in her mouth. She will then go headfirst up the other tree. Raccoon mothers have been seen to carry two babies at the same time, but this is unusual.

The raccoon's skin fits loosely around its muscular body. There are people who swear a coon can turn completely around inside its skin. This may be an exaggeration, but not as much as you might think. I have a friend who was fishing from a small boat when a raccoon came swimming past. Without thinking, my friend reached over, caught the coon by the fur in the middle of its back, and lifted it from the water.

That coon may not have turned completely around inside its skin, but somehow it turned enough to sink its teeth into my friend's forearm, even while he held it by the middle of the back. At this point my friend decided it was time to let the coon go, but now the coon refused. Raccoons have forty teeth, all sharp. Four of them, two upper and two lower, called canines, are unusually long and needle sharp. They can make a nasty wound. This raccoon kept biting and clawing until my friend plunged his arm, raccoon and all, under the water. Even then the coon held on for what seemed several hours. Finally it let go and swam off, making growling noises.

### Fur and Color

The color of the raccoon's fur, like its weight, may vary both with the individual and with the area in which it lives. Some are so dark as to be almost black. Some have a slight reddish tint. Even pure white albino coons have been found occasionally. On the whole, the darkest colored animals live in the Pacific Northwest. Desert raccoons in the Southwest have a yellowish tint. But the basic color of the average raccoon is brownish touched with tips of gray in places. The tail is slightly lighter in color than the body, and ringed with five to seven black stripes.

About 90 percent of the raccoon's fur is made up of a short,

*Back in the 1920s, raccoon coats such as this were so popular that coons were heavily hunted for their hides. In some areas the raccoons were almost wiped out. This is a recent picture of an old coat.*

soft underfur. The other 10 percent, called guard hairs, is much longer and coarser. Actually these are the hairs that give the raccoon most of its color, since these are the ones most clearly seen.

The raccoon's fur is wonderfully suited to the raccoon's way of life. Unfortunately for the coon, it has also been of value to men. As we have seen, Indians and frontiersmen used it for both clothing and cash money. But there were never enough Indians or frontiersmen to endanger the raccoon species. Shortly after World War I, however, long overcoats made of raccoon skins became popular with college boys and girls. As the demand increased, the price of coonskins went from one and two dollars each to nine or ten or more. As a result, coon hunting changed from being basically a sport into a business. Northern raccoons

26

have a heavier, thicker fur than southern coons and these brought better prices. Soon the raccoon was in danger of being wiped out in many northern areas.

Then the fashion changed. Raccoon coats were no longer popular. The price of the skins dropped. The hunting slowed— and very quickly the raccoons were as numerous as before.

Since the era of the coonskin coat, the popularity of raccoon fur has gone up and down. With the long guard hairs sheered off, raccoon fur can be very soft, pretty, and long lasting. But it has never again been so popular as to threaten the animal's existence.

# 5. The Raccoon's Senses

Seen by daylight a raccoon's eyes look like round balls of tar. They are so black they seem to have no pupils, though of course they do. But at night, caught in the glare of a bright light, these eyes glitter orange-red, or sometimes green. Some scientists believe that the longer a raccoon stares into a bright light, the redder the glow of its eyes.

This bright eye glow is caused by something called the *tapetum lucidum*, meaning "shining carpet" at the back of the eye. This is a film of mirrorlike cells built into the back of a raccoon's eye—and into the eyes of a number of animals that hunt chiefly by night. Raccoons can, and often do, hunt by daylight, but they are chiefly nocturnal. The purpose of the *tapetum lucidum* is to reflect any dim night light that has passed through the retina of the raccoon's eye without being used. In effect this gives the animal a chance to use some light twice and so improve its night vision.

The raccoon has excellent vision by day as well as by night. Strangely, however, raccoons seem to be color blind. They can tell a bright object from a dark one. But scientists experimenting with raccoons have been unable to get them to react to any actual color. Nor do they seem to rely very much on their sight to find food. Many times I have put out a bowl of food for the raccoons that live in the mangroves and cabbage palms near my

28

*This photograph was taken with a flash. Note the way the raccoon's eyes reflect the light.*

home. Often a coon will see me put down the plate, then will walk right past it until downwind from the food. Then it will stop, lift its head to smell, and follow its nose back to the food.

Raccoons also have excellent hearing. They probably hunt

for frogs, insects, and such small game as much by sound as by either smell or sight. Strangely, however, noise itself doesn't appear to bother a raccoon. The crashing of thunder that will terrify a dog doesn't trouble a pet raccoon. In the wild they have made their nests under railroad and highway bridges where trains and cars roared past day and night.

## A Washer? Or a Feeler?

Probably the raccoon's keenest sense, the one on which it relies most often, is its sense of touch, or feeling. The raccoon appears to gather much of its information about things in general, as well as its food, from this sense of touch.

*Procyon lotor*, you remember, got the last part of its scientific name because it was believed that it washed all its food before eating it, even a fish fresh out of the water. Indeed, there were some persons who said the raccoon had no salivary glands and that it was necessary for it to wet its food before it could swallow it. But Dr. Leon Whitney proved by both experiments and autopsies that raccoons have very active salivary glands.

However, it is true that a raccoon will often catch a small fish or a crab at the water's edge, kill it, and then dip it back in the water before eating.

If you give a young, pet raccoon a lump of sugar (coons love sweets) it is quite likely that he will immediately dip it into his water bowl. Using both hands, he will roll it carefully, gently, between them. When he lifts his hands out of the water and the sugar has disappeared he will stare at his empty paws in amazement.

But if this happens, it is probably the first lump of sugar this particular raccoon has ever had. Give him another lump and he will pop it promptly into his mouth without going near the water. Raccoons learn quickly. Also, they have no actual need to wet their food before eating. A coon feasting on sweet corn or

*A raccoon feeding in a garbage can*

wild grapes or out of someone's garbage can may be a half mile from water. Then he eats his food where he finds it. But if he is near water the raccoon may, and often does, dip his food into the water.

Just why raccoons have this curious habit no one can say for sure. Certainly it is not a matter of cleanliness. Put a pan of

*The raccoon may, or may not, dip food in the water before eating it. This one ate right where it was.*

clean water in a raccoon's pen alongside a pan of very muddy water and the coon is as likely to dip its food in one as the other. Some naturalists believe the raccoon simply likes to play in water. Some believe the wetness increases the raccoon's sense of touch. And certainly raccoons often seem to rely more on touch than on any other sense in hunting for their food.

Watch a raccoon hunting for crayfish, crabs, minnows, or whatever he can find along the edge of a lake or river. His tail may drag in the water behind him, but he is not using it for bait. He is hunting with his hands. His head is held high, and he is not watching the water. He seems to be gazing off into space, though perhaps he is actually looking out for enemies. Beneath the surface his hands move steadily, gently, causing barely a ripple. Then, suddenly, there is a flash of movement and he is out of the water carrying a fish or crab with him.

In Florida, commercial mullet fishermen often haul their nets in narrow, mangrove-lined bayous. Where they do, the wild raccoons soon come to understand what is happening. And sometimes a raccoon will drop out of a mangrove onto the stern of a fishing boat. There it sits. It does not watch the net being hauled over the stern. It may watch the fisherman, though frequently it seems to gaze off into space. It may be listening for the sound of a mullet flopping in the net. But always its sensitive, monkeylike hands are feeling the net as it comes in. And when its fingers find a fish they quickly, skillfully, lift it clear. Quickly the raccoon bites it below the head, breaking its spine. After this the coon may jump into the water, or into an overhanging mangrove, taking the fish with him.

It is the raccoon's remarkable front paws—I think, in the case of the raccoon, *hands* is really a better word than *paws*—that makes this possible. They are shaped very much like human hands. The raccoon does not have what is called an opposed thumb, as human beings do. But the three middle fingers are

32

*Raccoon prints in the mud*

much longer than the other two, and the two outside fingers work together across the middle three.

The toes of the raccoon's back feet are not quite as long as the fingers of the hands. They leave a print that looks very much like a human baby's foot, just as the front feet leave handlike prints. In fact, a collection of coon tracks on the soft bank of a creek or pond make it look as if the fairies had held a gathering.

It is truly amazing what a raccoon can do with those agile, sensitive hands. They not only hunt for food, they can untie knots, open doors and garbage cans. In a Florida park not long ago the campers complained that raccoons were getting into the garbage cans and littering trash about. (Raccoons are sloppy eaters.) So the park system bought special cans designed to be animal proof. "The trouble was," said one of the rangers later, "people couldn't open the cans, but the coons could."

Highly intelligent, raccoons often work together. Many times I have seen one raccoon inside my garbage can handing food out to another standing on its hind legs outside. A neighbor with a large garbage can watched one raccoon stand on the back of another to reach the lid and push it off. Once I tied the lid onto my garbage can in such a way that I figured no coon could ever get it off. I was awakened in the night by a loud crash. Looking out the window, I saw two raccoons rolling the can down the middle of the street. They rolled it for half a block until finally the lid did come off; then they stopped and ate dinner.

One of the strangest stories of coon teamwork is sworn to by a famous naturalist. He was camping and awoke to see two raccoons prowling softly around his fire. They found a jar of fruit, rolled it first one way, then the other, but the lid did not come off. Finally one raccoon picked up the jar and held it clutched to its chest with both arms. The other raccoon, using both hands, unscrewed the cap. Then both together ate the fruit.

But it is the raccoon's ability to open doors, particularly refrigerator doors, that has caused his human observers the most problems. Pet coons quickly learn where food is kept and how to reach it. Almost nothing short of a padlock will keep them out of drawers and cabinets that contain food. But what of the wild raccoon?

I have a friend who has a glassed-in porch on which he keeps a refrigerator. There is also a small, swinging door that allows his toy poodle to come and go at will. And the poodle's food is sometimes kept in the refrigerator. Wild raccoons often came in the yard, but none had ever been in the house. So he thought nothing of going away for a week, leaving the well-stocked refrigerator on the porch.

When he came home he found the refrigerator doors wide open. The porch and the yard outside were littered with scraps of food—and with what looked like tiny footprints and hand-

*Raccoons have remarkable paws. This pet is eating a watermelon that was cut open for him. But in the fields coons will claw melons open for themselves.*

prints. Raccoons had come in through the poodle's swinging door, opened the refrigerator door, and cleaned it out.

How could the wild raccoons have known there was food in the refrigerator? It would seem impossible that they could have smelled it. Probably they opened the doors out of mere curiosity and so found the food. All raccoons seem to be incurably curious. Or is it possible the wild raccoons wandering about the yard in the past had seen the refrigerator open, with food inside, and had remembered?

# 6. The Raccoon in Fall and Winter

It may seem strange to begin a year-round look at an animal with the fall rather than with the spring. But the raccoon is a strange animal anyway. In areas where there is little or no winter, raccoons feed and act pretty much the same, year around. But not in the North. Therefore, this section will deal chiefly with raccoons outside the Deep South.

In the North, as the days shorten and the nights turn chill, a kind of feeding frenzy comes over these raccoons. Even a well-fed pet will rush at its food, growling, and acting as if it were starving to death. The wild raccoon will begin its nightly hunt for food earlier than before, and hunt later. Indeed, many will be out well before darkness. Raccoons that live along the seashore never worry too much about day and night anyway. For them, hunting is best at low tide, and they hunt by the tide more than by the sun.

In the fall, nuts are most plentiful. The raccoons feed on acorns, hickory and beech nuts, pecans, almost anything except black walnuts, which have a shell too tough to crack. But nothing delights a raccoon more than a field of corn. Here its eating habits are at their sloppiest and most destructive. A coon will climb a cornstalk until it bends or breaks under its weight, then turn its attention to the ear. It rips back part of the shuck, gnaws at the corn, leaves it and attacks another ear. A single coon can

*A raccoon feeding on corn, a favorite food*

destroy an amazing amount of corn in a night. Also, at this time the female raccoon is still followed by her young born in the spring. They will be almost grown now, weighing about eight or nine pounds each, and just as hungry as their mother. When several families of raccoons move into a cornfield they can lay waste an acre or more, eating only a fraction of the corn they destroy.

Grapes, apples, and pears delight raccoons as well as corn. But as mentioned before, raccoons are not strict vegetarians. By late autumn most frogs may have disappeared, but field mice are often plentiful. The coons eat them happily. Crickets and grass-hoppers singing their farewell songs may never get to finish. And raccoons, like the bears they somewhat resemble, love honey. Apparently their thick fur prevents them from being stung. Anyway, a raccoon will plunge directly into a honey tree if it finds one, paying no heed to the enraged bees.

In the fall, a sixteen-pound raccoon will eat as much as three to four pounds of food a day, one quarter of its own weight. As it does, it naturally grows fat. The fat forms in thick layers underneath its fur. It may be as much as an inch thick. Even the coon's tail accumulates a layer of fat.

As the fat thickens, so does the coon's fur. It takes on a glossy look. This is the prime time of year for the raccoon's fur. And so it is the prime time of year for the men who hunt raccoons to sell their fur.

### THE DEN

Besides getting fat, the raccoon has one other important thing to do in the late fall. It must find a den for a winter home. The two jobs are closely related; later, as it sleeps away the coldest days and nights of winter, it must live on the stored fat of its autumn feeding.

In the wilderness the raccoon's favorite den is in a hollow tree. The entrance may be anywhere from ground level to seventy feet above ground. The doorway may be only four inches or so in diameter—it's amazing what a small entrance a fat raccoon can get through—but usually it is bigger.

The hollow inside the tree may be as small as two cubic feet, not very much bigger than the coon itself. Or it may extend for ten to twenty feet or more up the tree. Raccoons have been found nesting in hollow trees that had no tops, so the snow and rain fell directly on the sleeping animal. Usually, however, the raccoon's winter nest is quite well protected.

*Three five-week-old baby raccoons in a tree den*

As a rule, the raccoon does not bring in leaves, moss, and such things to line its nest. Instead, it claws and bites at the semirotten wood inside the hollow. This enlarges the den and also makes a soft bed.

In areas where no good hollow trees are available, raccoons must find some kind of replacement. They nest in the attics of houses and barns. They will move underground into the burrows of woodchucks or other animals. They will move into old drainpipes or wriggle far back in a pile of rock.

A Texas raccoon picked what has to be one of the oddest of all dens. Conservation officials had set up a number of nail-keg boxes to attract nesting wood ducks. One of these was on a post in a lake, a good twenty feet or more from land. A raccoon simply swam out, climbed the post, and settled down in the nail keg.

By the time the female raccoon decides on a winter den she is probably alone. All during the fall her youngsters have learned to hunt more and more on their own. One at a time they wander off and don't come back. Led by instinct, they hunt for dens of their own. On the other hand, a mother and several of her young have been known to den up together. Also, in early winter, before the mating season starts, several adults may den together. Whether this is for warmth or because of a lack of dens is uncertain. But where several den together, they get along without fighting.

When the raccoon does pick out its winter den it does not

*A raccoon may stir from his winter den on almost any warm day.*

immediately settle down for a long winter's nap. It may sleep during the day and part of the night, then go out to hunt for awhile, and back to bed. The tremendous appetite of the early fall has gone. Now the raccoon has started to live chiefly on its own fat. And as the days grow still shorter, the weather colder, the raccoon spends more and more time curled up in its den asleep.

The winter sleep of the raccoon is not a true hibernation like that of the woodchuck, the flying squirrel, and some other animals. In these animals the heartbeat becomes extremely slow. The body temperature drops until the animal will seem to be and feel as if it were dead. But the raccoon's temperature drops very little; the heartbeat slows, but only slightly. If the weather stays cold, the sky overcast and dark, the raccoon may sleep steadily for a month or even more. But on almost any warm day it may stir about, look out, even prowl around near its den. Raccoons don't like deep snow. Short-legged, they have trouble moving through it. Even so, the raccoon seems to prefer eating snow to drinking water during this time.

Usually it is around the first of December when the raccoon starts its winter sleep. This sleep ends about late March or whenever the real spring thaw begins. Strangely, however, there is always one sharp break in this semihibernation, and it may come when the winter is at its coldest.

## MATING

In the South, raccoons may mate in December or early January. Farther north, however, it is usually late January or February before the male raccoon grows restless in his sleep. It is not hunger that awakens him. There is still a layer of fat under his skin. But now he is driven by an urge he cannot resist: the instinctive need to find a mate.

It is nearly always the male that goes hunting. The female

remains in her den, waiting. It may be bitterly cold with deep snow on the ground. It does not matter. With early darkness the male climbs down from his den and starts searching. He goes from one tree to another. He may be guided by his knowledge of the area in which he lives, knowing already where the most likely den trees are located. Once near the tree it is probably his nose that tells him whether or not a female lives here.

Normally raccoons travel no more than a mile or so in one night while hunting for food. But the male raccoon searching for a female may keep going. Leonard Lee Rue, an excellent outdoor photographer, once followed the tracks of a male raccoon that had traveled eight miles through deep snow in one night.

The male raccoon will mate with any willing female that he finds. Not so the female. She may drive off one suitor after another, snarling, biting if necessary, until finally the male of her choice arrives.

Dr. Leon Whitney found that in captivity a female raccoon that had accepted a mate would then refuse any other male put in the pen with her. If the mate was put into another pen the female would make whimpering noises. If the pens were placed close together both the male and female would pace up and down, as near one another as possible. If the pens were side by side, each raccoon would reach through the wire to stroke the other's fur.

In the wild when the female accepts a male he usually moves into the den with her. He may stay for a few days, or a few weeks. Then, as a rule, he moves on, looking for another mate. The female goes back into her winter sleep. The male too will soon find a place to curl up and sleep until the first soft rains of spring begin.

# 7. The Raccoon in Spring and Summer

In early spring when the raccoon becomes fully awake all its autumn fat is gone. Much of its fur has been shed. This shedding starts at the head and works back toward the tail. The fur comes out in large patches and what is left looks dirty and scraggly. The raccoon's skin hangs loose against its skeleton. If the winter has been unusually long, or if the raccoon was not well fattened when it went to sleep, it may be on the verge of starvation. Driven by hunger, the coon may now search for food by daylight as well as at night.

At this time of the year the raccoon will instinctively eat the tips of new grass, the soft buds of plants, almost any new, growing thing it can find. Earthworms, crawling up through the rain-softened ground, make a good part of the raccoon's diet. Frogs, awake now from their own winter nap and singing love songs in search of mates, are eaten happily.

Probably it is at this time of the year that the raccoon's wasteful eating habits do the most harm. If a coon finds a quail's nest it will eat as many eggs as it wants. And then, quite likely, it will simply destroy the rest. This is difficult to understand. Many animals, having found a supply of food, will eat what they want at the time and save the rest for later. The raccoon will often destroy, apparently for pleasure, the very eggs that it might need the next day.

*Raccoons will not only steal and eat chicken eggs, they will eat the chickens if they can catch them.*

Where raccoons are plentiful they may threaten the survival of some other animals. In a North Carolina tidal marsh raccoons broke into more than 90 percent of the muskrat houses in a single year, eating the young. The adult muskrats were much too fast and agile for the coons to catch. Even so, within a five-year period, raccoons had reduced the muskrat population by almost 95 percent.

On Cape Sable in the Everglades National Park naturalists one spring carefully located the nests of 199 giant sea turtles. But before the turtle eggs could hatch, raccoons had destroyed 140 of those nests.

(There is a strange thing about those Cape Sable raccoons that nobody quite understands. On the Cape fresh water is almost nonexistent. However, there are a number of places where a well only one or two feet deep will reach water. In such places the Park Rangers often find holes apparently dug by the raccoons.

At least there are holes with water in them, surrounded by the tracks of raccoons. If the coons did not dig these shallow wells, then no one knows who did. Also, just to the north of Cape Sable, among the Ten Thousand Islands, many raccoons live on mangrove islands that are flooded daily by salt tides. Here there is no fresh water at all. But Park Rangers have seen these coons lick the dew from mangrove leaves. Apparently—though no one knows for sure—they get all the fresh water they need in this way.)

### The Young

As mentioned earlier, the female raccoon will sometimes go into her winter den along with other coons. These may be either other adults or some of her young from the previous spring. But now, in late March or early April, she becomes aware that once more she is going to bear young. For this she needs a den to herself. She will drive off, fighting if necessary, any other raccoons that have shared the den.

The gestation period—the time between her winter mating and the birth of the young—may vary from fifty-seven to sixty-three days. So in most of the country outside the Deep South, the majority of raccoons are born about the middle of April. There is one minor exception. Male raccoons are never sexually mature until they are two years old or more. However, some females will mate during the summer of their second year. When this happens the young are born fairly late in the year. There is little chance for them to gain enough fat to last through the winter, and many of the young born late in the year die of starvation during their first winter.

Called kits, the babies, whenever they are born, look quite a bit like baby rats. They only weigh about two ounces each. Their eyes are tightly shut. Although they are fully furred at birth, the black mask on the face and the rings on the tail are

*This baby raccoon was born in captivity. It is peeping out of the hollow log that was given to its mother for a den.*

rarely visible at this time. A litter may vary from two to seven, with an average of four to five.

During the first week or so of their lives the young do nothing but drink their mother's milk, learn gradually to crawl, and sometimes make loud, purring noises. Between the eighteenth and twenty-third day their eyes open. By this time they are crawling back and forth over one another in a wriggling jumble. Gradually the face mask and tail rings begin to show.

The nursing mother will usually lie on her side, as a cat or dog will do. The babies then crawl along beside her, playful as puppies, pushing one another away to get at a nipple. But as the young get older and stronger the mother may change her position. Sometimes she will sit with her back propped against the wall of the den. This is the position that bears often use to nurse their young. It may be one of the reasons that early naturalists, studying the raccoon, believed it to be related to the bear.

Male raccoons, given a chance, may kill and eat their own young. However, they rarely get such a chance, since the female protects her young and will drive any male, including the father, away. If for some reason the mother needs to change dens, she will carry her babies, one at a time in her mouth, to the new home. On the other hand, if she has borne her young in captivity and something happens to disturb her, she may kill and eat them herself. It is very important that the mother raccoon in captivity be left in peace and quiet.

The mother raccoon must leave her den occasionally in order to feed herself. However, she does this no more often than necessary. Also, she rarely brings food back to the den. As long as the babies stay in their nest, they live almost entirely on their mother's milk.

Young raccoons, like human beings, have two sets of teeth. The first, called milk teeth, are replaced by permanent teeth when the babies are about fourteen weeks old. And it is about this point that the young coons usually stop nursing and start to feed themselves.

All raccoons have very small gullets and must chew their food well before swallowing. This is particularly true of the baby coons. Give one a piece of bread, and it will sit on its haunches and chew and chew until the bread is no more than liquid.

Even before the young start to feed themselves they have begun to leave the den and follow their mother on her nightly hunts for food. This begins when the babies are about eight to ten weeks old. At this time they are playful as puppies and look a lot like teddy bears. Usually in single file, they follow their mother out of the den and, maybe headfirst, maybe tailfirst, start down the tree trunk.

At this point there may be trouble. All baby raccoons are natural climbers, but at first they find it easier to go up a tree than down it. So one baby may decide to go up rather than down—and keep going up until it reaches the top and can't go farther. Nor can it come down. Instead it sets up a loud whimpering until momma comes and either carries or helps it down the tree. On the ground, usually in single file with momma in

*All baby raccoons are natural climbers.*

the lead, the family sets off through the woods or along the edge of a pond where the mother hunts.

Momma Raccoon is a strict disciplinarian. Walking slowly, she makes a low, churring noise. Apparently this is meant to help the youngsters, following in the dark, keep their position. If they fail to do so, momma takes action. A. S. Leopold, a naturalist, once wrote of watching a mother raccoon with five youngsters travel along the bank of a pond on a moonlit night. Two of the babies wandered off into the bushes, became lost, and set up a loud whimpering. Immediately the mother turned back. She plunged into the bushes and drove the youngsters out, swatting them on their tails with almost every step. Back in the moonlight, they once more lined up single file and marched off.

Young raccoons often play at fighting one another. Growling and pawing, this play can get rough at times. Also, several may join together to pick on one of their brothers or sisters. Then momma will rush into the middle of the fight, swatting right and left, until order is restored.

In following their mother night after night, the young gradually learn to feed themselves. By the time their milk teeth are gone, they can find bird eggs for themselves and catch their own frogs and crayfish. Sometimes, however, the lessons are more complicated. Late one afternoon I caught a two-pound catfish in the canal in front of my house and dropped it on the dock. Within moments a young raccoon came out of the mangroves and moved toward the fish. The catfish, still very much alive, lashed back and forth. Its long, barbed spines could have blinded or seriously injured the young raccoon and it seemed instinctively to know this. It backed away from the fish, then stopped. It knew the fish represented food but didn't know how to get it.

At this point the mother raccoon, followed by three other youngsters, came out of the mangroves. The mother did not pause. She walked around the catfish so that she came at it from the back. With a single move, almost as quick as a striking snake, she bit it just back of the head, breaking its spine. Carrying the fish in her mouth, she went back into the mangroves, followed by her young. There she stopped, holding the fish until it was completely motionless before she put it down for all of them to eat.

### Summer

As spring turns into summer the raccoon adjusts its diet to fit the season. Ponds and roadside puddles are apt to be swarming with tadpoles. This gives the coon not only a chance to feast, but to splash happily in the water at the same time. Plants are bigger and more numerous than in the early spring; coons frequently raid gardens for peas, potatoes, and the early corn they so dearly love. Seashore raccoons feast on clams and oysters, gnawing at the hinge of the shell until it pops open.

By midsummer the babies are half grown, or more, looking exactly like their parents. They still follow momma on her nightly hunts, but with growing independence. The adult males hunt chiefly alone. If the male meets the female with which he mated during the winter, they appear to recognize one another. Generally, there is a touching of noses, sniffing, and then each goes on its own way.

Each adult male, like each female with her family, has its own territory which it knows and rarely leaves. These territories may overlap, particularly if there is an area where garbage cans or other food is plentiful. But each raccoon, or family of raccoons, stays fairly well in its own area. I once had an old coon with the habit of climbing up on the windowsill about three feet from my dining room table. There she sat every evening, staring in at my wife and me until I quit eating my dinner and went out to feed her.

This would have been all right except that she always arrived wet and muddy from walking through the mangroves. She left the white wall of the house smeared with mud that had to be washed off daily. Finally my wife rebelled. I was ordered to trap the coon and take her elsewhere.

The place I released her was a full five miles from my home, in an area where food was plentiful. But two days later when I sat down for dinner I looked out the window. The old coon was sitting there staring at me.

This time I took her fifteen miles away, completely off the island and across the bay. She never came back.

*Raccoons may come to visit.*

In their nightly travels around their home territory some raccoons learn more than the location of dens and food. In an excellent book called *Raccoons Are the Brightest People*, Sterling North tells about one old raccoon that lived near a friend of his. This old coon often came to the house, pushed open the screen door, and came into the kitchen to be fed. Then one night North's friend was playing Beethoven's Ninth Symphony on his phonograph. The music had been on for only a few minutes when the kitchen door opened. The old raccoon came in, padded softly across the kitchen into the living room, and lay down on the floor in front of the phonograph. He stayed there until the music ended, got up, and went out into the night again.

After that, North's friend noticed that whenever he played Beethoven's Ninth Symphony, the old raccoon came in to listen. But he never came for any other music.

51

# 8. Raccoon Noises

Raccoons may not be able to talk the way some parrots can, but certainly they can make a weird and wild variety of noises.

One night not long ago I heard a lot of twittering, chirping, churring sounds coming from a big rubber tree near my home. It was much like the noise made by a flock of sparrows as they settle down for the night, but also there was a harsher sound. I turned the beam of a large flashlight into the tree—and suddenly it seemed filled with brilliant, round, golden eyes shining back at me.

There must have been twelve or more raccoons in that tree— probably three or four mothers with their young—and all of them making noises. But what they were so noisy about, I couldn't find out.

A mother coon with her young walking behind her will often make a low churring noise that seems intended to help the youngsters follow her. The young will make occasional soft noises of their own, like those of a child talking to itself. But all these noises can change instantly to take on a new meaning.

If a young coon starts to wander away from the family, or to investigate something the mother considers dangerous, the mother makes a sharp, grunting sound. It sounds almost as if a person tried to say "No!" loudly with his lips shut. Apparently it means "No!" and almost always the youngster quickly obeys.

52

*A happy raccoon can make a purring noise much like that of a cat, but louder.*

If one doesn't, the mother adds a violent swat with her paw to her grunting.

A happy raccoon can make a purring noise much like that of a cat, but louder. Raccoons like to sunbathe, and one stretched out on a tree limb in the sun may make a purring noise so loud it sounds as if the raccoon had left a motor running inside itself. A tame coon that likes to be petted (some do, and some don't) will make this purring noise when having its neck rubbed.

Baby raccoons left by their mother for awhile and grown

hungry will make small, whimpering sounds much like that of a human baby.

During the mating season male raccoons will often fight one another. Such fights usually start with each male lowering his head almost to the ground, ears tight against his skull, his back humped even higher than usual. Each makes a loud, hissing noise, plainly intended to tell the other to get out of the area or there's going to be trouble. Then the two leap at one another, clawing, biting—and squalling. The noise is much like that of two cats fighting and can be heard a hundred yards or more. Often I've thought there were two cats battling in my yard when it turned out to be raccoons.

Some naturalists believe that raccoons can make as many as fourteen to fifteen distinctly different sounds, each with a meaning of its own. Certainly there is one sound, sharply different from all the others, and to which every coon within hearing seems to react instantly and instinctively. This is a scream—there is no other word for it—thin and terrifying. Apparently it means "Leave wherever you are and run for your lives!"

Dr. Leon Whitney once found a barrel which five adult raccoons were using as a den. The raccoons refused to leave the barrel, and each time Dr. Whitney reached inside, the coons snarled and bit at his hand.

Dr. Whitney tied a noose in a piece of rope, dropped it over the head of one raccoon, and started to pull it out of the barrel. The coon screamed. Instantly the other four leaped out of the barrel and fled.

Raccoon hunters have often heard and seen similar actions in the woods. Dogs may chase several raccoons into one tree, then stand baying beneath it. The hunter then may shake one of the coons out of the tree onto the ground where the dogs attack it. The coon screams. Instantly every other raccoon in the tree will leap to the ground and run.

*A raccoon chased by dogs will usually climb a tree. If shaken out and attacked by the dogs, it may scream a warning to other raccoons.*

Some raccoon hunters claim they can "call" raccoons out of their hiding places. This is partially true. The hunter makes a noise like that of a raccoon's scream. If it is made truly enough, the chances are that every coon within hearing will leave wherever it is and run for another hiding place.

Most naturalists believe this reaction to the scream is an instinctive reaction for the preservation of the species. If animals are threatened, but all run at the same time, then some are almost certain to escape. But if all tried to stay hidden, they might all be destroyed one at a time.

# 9. The Smart Raccoon

In his book *Raccoons Are the Brightest People*, Sterling North tells the true story of a female raccoon that developed the habit of going each night to the kitchen door of a certain house, hoping to be fed. The lady of the house liked coons; sometimes, however, she would be in another part of the house where she could not see or hear her visitor. The raccoon could not open the big, solid kitchen door. So at such times the coon was turned away hungry.

The lady decided to try an experiment. Just over the kitchen door she tied a fried chicken leg to a cord fastened to a bell. The coon stood on its hind legs, reached for the chicken leg, and in this way rang the bell. This was repeated several nights in a row. Then the lady left the cord hanging at the door, but with no food tied to it. The raccoon looked the situation over, reached up, and rang the bell anyway. The lady opened the door, let the coon into the kitchen, and fed it.

Again this practice was followed for several nights. Then one night the lady let the raccoon into the kitchen even before it rang the bell. She went to the refrigerator, took out food, but held it well out of the raccoon's reach. "Go ring the bell," she said.

The order had to be repeated. The lady had to go touch the bell cord, but eventually the raccoon got the idea. It went outside, rang the bell, came back in, and was fed. After this it would always ring the bell on order.

This practice went on all one summer and fall. Then the raccoon disappeared into its winter den. But it was back in the spring, followed by four babies. And one by one the mother raccoon taught them to ring the bell for dinner.

Almost everybody who has lived around raccoons has a story of this sort to illustrate their intelligence. And recently scientists have been working with raccoons trying to learn just how smart they really are.

In one test the raccoon had to open a number of different doors in order to reach its food. Each door was fastened with a latch that opened in a different way. After 107 different tries, the raccoon had learned to open all the doors without any mistakes.

For several weeks the raccoon had to open these doors every day in order to reach its food. It made no mistakes. Then the doors were taken away and the raccoon was fed normally. This

*Wild raccoons will quickly learn to go where they will be fed. This picture was taken by a neighbor of mine in his backyard where he fed raccoons every night.*

*It is best not to let a raccoon, even a pet one, take food from your fingers —unless you know the coon well and it knows you. This one is being fed by friend and owner.*

went on for a full year, then the puzzle was replaced. This time, after only twenty-four mistakes, the raccoon was able to open all the doors without error. Obviously the raccoon was not only able to learn, but to remember for a year at least part of that information.

In another test only two doors were used. Now the food was placed first behind one door, then behind the other, never behind the same door twice in a row. If the raccoon forgot and went to the wrong door, it got no food. Most of the coons tested learned quickly. Even when they were fed only once in twenty-four hours the old raccoons would remember from day to day. In fact, the scientist wrote, the old raccoons would remember sometimes when he had forgotten. On the other hand, young raccoons were apt to forget within twenty-four hours.

The scientific testing showed that raccoons, like people, differ one from another. Some learned more quickly than others, some forgot more quickly. Some raccoons got angry at being tested and tried to bite the person testing them. Indeed, some raccoons threw temper tantrums much like those of children. One scientist told of a raccoon that tried to climb the curtain in his laboratory. The curtain fell, tangling the coon. And the coon became furious, biting and clawing the curtain. Another coon fell off a trapeze on which it had been placed. It jumped up, climbed back on the trapeze, and tried to bite the ropes in two.

One laboratory raccoon liked to bite people on the ankle, apparently as a kind of game. This raccoon could be handled without trouble. It enjoyed being petted. But placed on the floor, it would slip up behind anyone who was not watching, nip them on the ankle, and run like crazy.

As a result of their tests most naturalists now believe that the raccoon may not be as intelligent as some species of monkeys and some porpoises. But certainly it is among the most intelligent of all animals.

# 10. Coon Hunting

Indians and pioneers hunted the raccoon for very practical reasons: they ate the meat and used the hides for clothing. As mentioned earlier, there was a time in the 1920s when, because of the popularity of its fur, the raccoon was hunted almost to extinction in some northern states. Even now there are many places where, every October and November, the raccoon is hunted for the value of its fur. Today the long, coarse guard hairs are often sheared off the fur, leaving the soft undercoat more visible. Such furs are both beautiful and long lasting.

But even when men depended on the raccoon for meat and clothing there were hunters with another and entirely different motive. This had nothing to do with the actual capture and killing of the animal. Instead, it was a kind of sport that depended largely on an ear for strange music, a love of natural beauty, and an appreciation of friendship. Today there are probably as many coon hunters of this kind as those who hunt only for the value of the dead animal.

Coon hunting is normally done at night when the raccoons themselves are out searching for food. It is rarely done alone, since its chief joys are friendship and conversation. Instead, two or more men go into the woods, taking their dogs with them. These dogs are an essential part of the hunt. They may be red-bone hounds, or bluetick hounds, or black-and-tan, but they

*Coon hunting is normally done at night when the raccoons themselves are out searching for food.*

have been bred and trained for coon hunting only. In an area where raccoons are likely to be found the dogs are released. The men sit down to wait. If the night is cold they may build a small fire. Moon and stars move slowly overhead. There may be no sound at all, or maybe the rustle of wind in the trees. The men talk quietly, but always they are listening for the first cry of the dogs.

Sometimes the dogs do not give voice. One by one they come back to the fire, shaking their heads as if to say, "No coons around here." Then the party moves to another part of the woods. Once more the dogs are released. Another small fire is built.

Suddenly one of the dogs bays. Every coon hunter knows the

voice of every one of his dogs. "That's old Lobo," one of the men says. "He's hit a trail."

Another dog joins in. "That's Miss Jeannie," its owner says.

Then another dog and another, until the whole pack is in full cry. This is the music the hunters have come for. To the men who love their dogs and hunting, it is as beautiful as any symphony. It is the main reason for being here on a cold night under the moon and stars. And to the listening men the voices tell the story of the hunt.

"The coon has doubled back on them," one man will say.

"He's heading for Parker's woods, going fast now," another says.

The voices of the hounds swell or fade as they come closer or go farther from the waiting men. For awhile one dog leads the pack, then another. Sometimes the voices stop for awhile. "That coon's swimming downstream in Jackson Creek," one of the hunters says. "But Old Red will pick him up when he comes ashore."

Then the baying starts again. "I told you Old Red would find him."

An experienced coon hunter can tell a great deal from the voices of the dogs, picturing the chase in his mind almost as if he could actually see it. Even so, the real chase may sometimes be different from the hunter's picture. The dogs may have struck the trail a mile or more behind the raccoon. The coon may hear them begin to bay; but the baying of dogs is common and the raccoon has no way of knowing it is his trail they follow. He continues to amble slowly along, hunting for insects, nuts, ripe fruit, anything he can find. He may come to a creek and wade along the edge, not trying to lose the dogs but to find food.

As the voices of the hounds come closer, the raccoon becomes more aware of them. He increases his pace. And once the raccoon realizes it is his trail the dogs are following, he calls on all his intelligence and strength to escape.

*A raccoon will often climb a tree to escape the hounds.*

Raccoons do not seem to be built for speed. With their high hips, they look awkward as they run. But Leon Whitney once followed one in an automobile down a road at twenty miles an hour. They have been known to run for a mile or more across open fields so swiftly that the following hounds gained ground only slowly.

Even so, the raccoon cannot match the speed and endurance of a pack of hounds. If there are trees nearby the normal thing is for the coon to climb one and remain there where the dogs cannot reach him. In a country where there are few trees the coon may hide in a rocky cliff or a badger hole. But sometimes there are neither trees nor holes close by and the coon must rely on cunning to keep ahead of the dogs. It may run upstream along the bank of a creek, turn and run back over its old tracks, then leap into the water and swim downstream, coming out on the far side of the creek. Sometimes the raccoon seems to make a

*A raccoon may swim away to avoid coon hunters and their dogs.*

game of the whole chase. It may climb a tree, but instead of staying there above the dogs, it will go from the limbs of that tree to another, and another, as far as possible. Then it will come down to the ground and run again.

If a pack of hounds catches the raccoon on the ground, they will kill it. But the raccoon is a fierce fighter. If the fight is between one raccoon and one hound, the odds are about even unless the dog is unusually big, strong, and experienced. However, it is always the dog that forces the fight. Given a chance, the raccoon will run.

If a fight between the raccoon and a single hound takes place in the water, the raccoon will nearly always win. The coon is the better swimmer and faster in the water. It will climb on top of the dog's head and hold it under water until it drowns. Even against two or more dogs the raccoon has a chance in the water, unless the dogs have learned to fight together.

Most coon hunts, however, do not end in fights between raccoon and hounds. Usually, as the dogs get closer and closer, the raccoon will climb a tree and stay there.

The hunters, listening by their fire, quickly know when the coon has treed: the voices of the hounds change suddenly. Now it is no longer the deep, musical baying of the chase but a shorter, barking noise. "He's treed," the hunters say to one another. They put out their fire and start walking toward the sound of the dogs.

If the coon is being hunted for its fur, one hunter will shine a flashlight into the tree where the coon hides. The coon's eyes will glow like great rubies. Strangely, raccoons never seem to be troubled by light shining on them at night. If anything, they seem attracted by it. Even a raccoon hunting along the edge of a pond will turn and stare into a light that shines suddenly on him. Often he may actually move toward it. Or, after a moment, he may go back to his hunting. Usually a treed coon stares down into the light, unmoving, and the hunters may shoot it.

If the coon is being hunted simply for the sport and not for its fur, the dogs may be called off, the raccoon left unharmed. Many ardent coon hunters, however, try to capture alive any female raccoons they have treed. To do this, usually two or more hunters will hold a net under the tree. Another will climb the tree and try to shake the limb on which the raccoon clings until it falls into the net. From the net it is quickly put into a heavy bag.

Such captured female raccoons are kept in pens to breed, then released with their young in the fall for more hunting. In this way a hunter may keep his favorite woods well stocked with raccoons.

# 11. The Russian Raccoon

In 1936 the Soviet government decided to learn if the adaptable raccoon could adapt itself to the Russian countryside. The idea was that if the raccoon could live there and multiply, it would become a valuable source of fur. Twenty-two coons were taken from a Russian zoo and turned loose in a forest near the Black Sea. The next year four more were released from a zoo. By 1950 slightly more than one hundred raccoons had been released in various forests.

The adaptable American raccoon promptly adapted itself to Russia. But even for the raccoon there were problems. The summer of 1951 was extremely dry in the area where most of the coons had been released. Ponds and lakes dried up. Rivers quit flowing, turned into small pools with dry spaces between them. Then the pools dried, one by one. The raccoons began to die.

There was still water in the nearby mountains, and the raccoons that were strong enough climbed the mountains. But in these high elevations there was still snow on the ground and the short-legged coon doesn't like snow. Even so, many survived. With autumn, new snow began to fall. The snowdrifts grew deeper and the raccoons moved back down the mountains, a little at a time, keeping ahead of the worst snow. At the lower elevations the snow turned to rain. The lakes refilled; rivers began to flow again. The raccoons fattened themselves as best

*The short-legged raccoon doesn't like deep snow.*

they could, then denned up for the winter. With spring, they were once more leading normal lives.

In many parts of northern Russia the winters are too long, the snow and ice too deep for the raccoon to survive. But between 1936 and 1958 the Soviet government released 1,243 raccoons into areas where it was believed the animal could live. However, most of these coons were not taken from zoos. They were the offspring of raccoons that had been released earlier, then trapped and moved to new areas.

By 1954 these few animals had multiplied to where the government allowed them to be hunted for their fur. But even though hunted, by 1964 there were an estimated 45,000 wild raccoons in Russia. Another five thousand or more had spread into East Germany, and the population was steadily increasing. The adaptable raccoon had done it again.

# 12. The Raccoon's Relatives

Scientists no longer believe the raccoon to be closely related to the bear. It does, however, have a relative that looks like a bear. And although the raccoon is strictly American (except where imported, as in Russia) this relative is Asiatic—the giant panda, *Ailuropoda melanoleuca*.

Actually, the giant panda looks more like a black-and-white teddy bear than a real animal. Weighing anywhere between 75 and 250 pounds, it may be as big as the average bear, but it looks more cuddly than frightening. Both its front and back legs are all black, and there is a black stripe across the shoulders. Everything else is shiny white—except the ears, eyes, and nose. These are black like the legs.

The giant panda lives in bamboo forests of southcentral China. Quite rare, very little is known about its life in the wild except that it feeds almost entirely on the roots and new growth of the bamboo. In fact, until 1929, naturalists in the Western world weren't even sure such an animal existed. Then Theodore and Kermit Roosevelt, sons of President Theodore Roosevelt, killed one on a hunting trip and brought its skin to the Chicago Natural History Museum. Later another panda was captured alive and taken to the Chicago Zoological Park. Named Su-Lin, it lived only two years. But during that time she was the star of the park.

*A giant panda at the Bronx Zoo*

Still later, a few more giant pandas were placed in zoos. Wherever one has appeared, it has always been the main attraction.

The giant panda is not the raccoon's only Asiatic relative. There are, in fact, two pandas: the giant black-and-white panda and the lesser, or red, panda, *Ailurus fulgens*. They don't look much alike, and neither one looks like a raccoon, but all three belong to the scientific family called Procyonidae. Naturalists divide this into two subfamilies: the Procyoninae, which includes the raccoon and its American relatives, and the Alurinae, the Asiatic pandas.

This lesser, or red, panda is not as cute looking as its big relative, and by no means as charming. About twenty to twenty-three inches long, not counting another foot and a half of bushy tail, it looks somewhat like an overgrown cat. Most of its fur is soft, red, and beautiful. The ears, eyes, and nose are ringed with white. The legs, underparts, and the tip of the tail are black. It is, in fact, much prettier than it is lovable. Although it can be partially tamed, it hates to be touched. Try to pat one and it is likely to bite viciously or strike with razor-sharp claws.

Like its giant relative, not much is known about its life in the wild. It lives in parts of China and in the high Himalaya Mountains. During the day it sleeps curled up in a hollow tree or on a tree limb. At night it feeds on bamboo sprouts, roots, grass, and other plants.

### THE CRAB-EATING RACCOON

Probably the closest relative of *Procyon lotor* is *Procyon cancrivorus*, the crab-eating raccoon of South America. Even so, it doesn't look or behave very much like its North American relative. The crab-eater, as its name implies, lives along river banks and seashores where crabs, and other marine animals, are plentiful. It has longer legs than *Procyon lotor*; its fur is brick red with white-fringed ears and a white nose. But it does have the raccoon mask and a ringed tail. But the tail is ringed black and white.

Not a great deal is known about the crab-eater, except that it seems almost as much at home in the water as on the shore. It has been seen as much as four miles from land, casually swimming across a bay or inlet of the open sea. If bothered, it makes a noise even stranger than any of those of *Procyon lotor*; this is a long, thin, whistling sound, so high-pitched it is almost out of the range of human ears.

### THE RING-TAILED CAT

The ring-tailed cat, *Bassariscus astutus*, is more ringed tail than cat. Its body is rarely more than a foot long, and no bigger

*A ring-tailed cat*

around than a squirrel's. Its bushy tail is every bit as thick as its body and almost half again as long. Ringed with vivid black-and-white stripes, it looks even bigger than it is. The body is a brownish-buff color on the back, black and white underneath. It has ears so big they look like wings. And to finish the picture, these stand straight up above a small foxlike face.

The ring-tail is fairly common from the northwest United States to southern Mexico. On the other hand, it is rarely seen. Like its raccoon relative, it feeds chiefly at night, spending the days curled up in hollow trees, or hidden in rocky ledges. It can squeeze through cracks that don't look big enough for a large fly. And startled, it can move so fast you can't be sure if you saw an animal or a shadow.

Like the raccoon, the ring-tail will eat just about anything it can find. It eats plants, insects, worms, and small animals, including birds. An excellent climber, it often catches birds asleep at night. On a happier note—for me, at least—it also catches mice. Captured young, ring-tails make excellent pets. Pioneers often kept them just to clean up the mice and rats.

### The Coatimundis

Coatimundis, or coatis—they go by both names—belong to the scientific genus *Nasua*. There are thought to be three species, each with its own last name to keep it apart from the others. *Nasua narica* can be found from the southwestern United States into South America. *Nasua nasua* lives throughout most of South America. And *Nasua nelsoni*, strangely, has never been found anywhere except on Cozumel, an island off the coast of Yucatan. Basically, all are much alike, the fur a dark reddish brown on the back and lighter underneath.

*A coatimundi*

Beyond that it is not easy to describe *Nasua*. A zoo visitor once shook his head and declared, "That animal looks like a little bit of everything." Ernest Thompson Seton, who was both an excellent artist and naturalist, said the coati was "a mixture of coon and monkey, with not a little dash of pig." To make matters worse, even a single species may vary in color from one area to another.

The "dash of pig" that Seton referred to is in the snout. This is so long that some persons have compared it to an elephant's trunk. It can be twitched from side to side and is used to root among leaves and soft earth for insects, plants, lizards, and other food. It also contains some needle-sharp teeth that make it a vicious fighter when it needs to be.

The coati is about the size of a raccoon and has a ringed tail. But the tail is much more like that of a monkey than that of a raccoon. It is every bit as long as the animal's body and usually carried straight up with just the tip curled over, like a question mark. As pets, coatis are playful as puppies. But left in a room unwatched, one is more than likely to tear down the drapes, open and empty the drawers, and turn over everything that can be turned over.

# 13. The Raccoon as a Pet

In a very good book called *Raccoons and Eagles*, Polly Redford wrote that raccoons never make good pets. They make interesting pets, she said. They make fascinating, funny, exciting pets. But they never make *good* pets—because raccoons are just naturally bad.

They are also smart. They can be trained to do almost anything—anything the raccoon wants to do. Sometimes this includes being housebroken, and sometimes it doesn't. And it never, never includes being quiet, placid, and dependable when left alone. Remember that by its nature the raccoon must touch, feel, rub almost everything it comes in contact with. One naturalist wrote that *Procyon lotor*, "the washer," should have been named *Procyon tengador*, "the feeler." Left in a house, he will climb the shelves to investigate the bright dishes and glassware, knocking over a few if not pulling down the shelves. He will quickly learn where the food is kept, and it is almost impossible to keep him from getting to it, ripping open boxes, emptying the refrigerator, spreading things around generally. He will learn how to turn on the water in the bathtub and lavatory—but I've never heard of a coon that knew how to turn it off. He likes to swing on the drapes, and his sharp claws will rip them if they don't fall down. He will burrow in between the pillows on the sofa. Then he will burrow *into* the pillows. He isn't trying to be destruc-

*Coons are playful.*

tive. He's just curious. He wants to know what's inside.

As a pet, raccoons should be kept outside except when carefully watched.

### CARE FOR THE YOUNG

There are a few "coon ranches" where raccoons are raised for sale. If you are buying a raccoon as a pet, be sure it is somewhere between one month and three to four months old. A coon less than a month old needs to be treated like a very young baby—a lot of trouble. A grown raccoon, raised in the wild, is almost impossible to tame. When raised in captivity it is apt to become attached to the original owner and resent a new one. So the best age is after the eyes are fully open, but before it is fully grown.

The truth is, however, not many persons buy raccoons for pets. Most coon owners get them by accident. A tree blows down in an early summer storm, and spills out a family of baby coons. Or a mother coon is killed by an automobile, leaving the babies tottering behind her. Polly Redford got hers when they fell through the ceiling onto the living room sofa—the mother raccoon had made her den in the Redford attic.

If you get a raccoon in this way and its eyes are not yet open, then you have work ahead. A very young coon needs to be fed every two to four hours, day and night. Mix one ounce of milk with two ounces of boiled water and five drops of Karo syrup. This can be fed to the raccoon with an eyedropper. Or you can suck a little of it into a straw, then let it run down into the baby coon's mouth. But the feeding has to go on round the clock. And the youngster will need a well-wrapped jar of hot water in its bed to help keep it warm.

By the time its eyes are well open and its teeth beginning to show, just plain milk, given less often, will do. Then you can start adding baby foods. As mentioned before, raccoons eat almost anything that people eat—except maybe tomatoes; they don't seem to like tomatoes. By the time the baby is three to four months old it should be completely weaned.

*Raccoons are just naturally curious. These two wild raccoons are studying an automobile left parked in the woods.*

*A baby raccoon, born in captivity, (left) investigates the den furnished by its owners. The raccoon and the dog are natural enemies. But when raised together (right) raccoons and dogs may become fast friends.*

As feeding becomes less of a problem, keeping it confined becomes more of a problem. You'll need some kind of cage, because even a two-month-old raccoon can climb out of almost any box. And already it's old enough to start swinging on the curtains and messing up the floor. Soon it will be best to move coon and cage outdoors. Remember that in natural circumstances it would be living outside. Even so, the cage must contain a box or something that can be used for a den where it can sleep and stay warm. Also it must be large enough to let the growing raccoon get exercise.

In the wild, dogs and raccoons are natural enemies. But a puppy and a baby raccoon raised together can become fast friends. If anything, the young coon is more playful than the puppy. It seems to have more energy and will keep teasing, nipping, pulling on its playmate after the puppy wants only to rest.

Often the friendship of dog and coon will last as long as the two stay together with no long separation. One man wrote about a dog and raccoon raised together until both were mature. One day the owner watched the two playing together in the yard. The dog, growing weary, came to the house door but couldn't get in. After a few moments it went back to the raccoon and touched noses, apparently saying something in animal language. The raccoon came to the house, stood on its hind legs, turned the door knob with its paws, pushed the door open. The dog went in, and the coon went back into the yard. Later the man saw this happen on several occasions.

### Farewell to the Pet

The owner of a pet raccoon must be prepared for problems and grief as well as pleasure. As mentioned earlier, raccoons may get a variety of diseases. In very cold areas it is sometimes difficult to give the pet a proper den for the winter. And despite its intelligence, the raccoon that's allowed to roam is not as good as most dogs and cats at avoiding automobiles. The automobile is probably the raccoon's most deadly enemy.

Also, even though raised in captivity from babyhood, the raccoon is by nature a wild animal. Some are much easier to tame, much more affectionate than others. Some never really adjust

*Though raised in captivity, the raccoon is by nature a wild animal.*

to a life with human beings. Even affectionate coons may act on a sudden, wild impulse. Leonard Lee Rue, the photographer, once reached up to take a pet coon off his shoulder. The coon didn't want to get down. It bit Rue on the ear, its teeth passing completely through his ear. Then it held onto his neck with its paws. It didn't mean to hurt; it only wanted to stay where it was. But its sharp claws left deep cuts.

It is best, always, to handle a pet raccoon with care, being sure not to startle or frighten it.

Perhaps the greatest problem, the greatest sorrow, facing the owner of a pet raccoon is the fact that very probably he must lose it within one or two years. Now and then a raccoon will adjust to life in captivity and never try to run wild. But this is rare. As the raccoon ages, its natural, wild instincts increase. The sexually mature raccoon wants a mate. Kept in its cage, it will make loud, screeching, screaming noises. It may pace back and forth until its feet become raw. Released, it goes looking for a mate wherever it may find one.

The pet raccoon that has been released may return home now and then, sometimes only for a quick meal, sometimes for a day or two. But almost never will it once again become a true pet.

Sterling North in his book *Rascal* tells of when he had to let his much loved pet go free. With Rascal in the bow, North rowed his canoe down a creek to where the forest began. There they drifted quietly for awhile. It was night, a full moon shining. From the creek bank came the soft call of a female raccoon. Rascal turned toward it. Then he looked back at his master. For a full minute the raccoon hesitated, uncertain. Then he made his decision. He dived over the side and swam ashore. He never came back.

In raccoon ranches the animals may be kept and bred in cages for a number of years. But these are not true pets. For the raccoon owner who loves his pet, the time will almost certainly come when he must let it go back to the wild.

# Index